Joy Dermott

09

PICTURE A COUNTRY

France

Henry Pluckrose

W

FRANKLIN WATTS
LONDON·SYDNEY

This is the French flag.

First Published in 1998
by Franklin Watts
This edition 2001

Franklin Watts
96 Leonard Street
London EC2A 4XD

Franklin Watts Australia
56 O'Riordan Street
Alexandria, Sydney
NSW 2015

© Franklin Watts 1998

ISBN 0 7496 4289 0

A CIP catalogue record for this book is
available from the British Library

Dewey Decimal Classification Number: 914..4

10 9 8 7 6 5 4

Series Editor: Rachel Cooke
Designer: Kirstie Billingham
Picture research: Juliet Duff

Printed in Dubai

Photographic acknowledgements:

Cover: Robert Harding Picture Library t and bl,
James Davis Travel Photography br.

AKG, London p. 29t;
J. Allan Cash pp. 15, 19t, 24;
Allsport p. 26;
Axiom Photographic Agency pp. 19b, 20, 23 (D. Shaw);
Cephas p. 18 (Mick Rock);
James Davis Travel Photography p. 12, 22;
Eye Ubiquitous p. 29b;
Getty Images pp. 9 (Manfred Mehlig), 10 (Joe Cornish),
20-21 (Tony Craddock);
Robert Harding Picture Library pp. 8, 13, 14, 16, 17, 21b,
27, 28.
Images Colour Library p. 11;
Travel Ink p. 25.

All other photography Steve Shott.
Map by Julian Baker.

Contents

GREAT BRITAIN

ENGLISH CHANNEL

BELGIUM

GERMANY

BRITTANY

Paris

River Seine

Carnac

Le Mans

Strasbourg

River Loire

FRANCE

SWITZERLAND

ATLANTIC
OCEAN

River
Gironde

Chamonix

Lyon

The Alps

ITALY

River
Rhône

Puy-L'Eveque

Toulouse

Pyrenees Mountains

Marseilles

Menton

SPAIN

MEDITERRANEAN SEA

CORSICA

Where is France?

This is a map of France.
France is the largest country in western Europe.
The island of Corsica in the Mediterranean Sea
is also part of France.

Here are some
French stamps
and old French
money called
francs. France has
now replaced
francs with Euros.

The French landscape

France is a country of plains,
hills and mountains.
Several great rivers flow through France,
including the Loire, the Rhône and the Seine.

This train travels through the high French Alps near Chamonix.

In northern France the weather is warm in summer and cool and wet in the winter.
In southern France, the weather is hotter and drier throughout the year.

The French people

People have lived in France for many, many thousands of years.

People put up the ancient stones at Carnac in Brittany between three and four thousand years ago.

The long lines of stones at Carnac were probably put up by ancient people as part of their religion.

The Pont du Gard in southern France was built by the Romans to carry water from one place to another.

Two thousand years ago France was part of the Roman Empire.

Today over 58 million people live in France.

Where they live

Marseilles is on the Mediterranean. It is France's second largest city, with over a million people living there.

If you were French, you might live in a busy seaport like Marseilles, an industrial town like Lyon or the city where the European Parliament gathers, Strasbourg.

Instead of a city, you might live in a peaceful village or small town surrounded by woods and fields.

This is the small town of Puy-L'Evêque in the south-west of France.

The capital city

The Eiffel Tower is over 300 metres high.
It is one of the best-known sights of Paris.

Tourists often see Paris by boat.
This boat is passing Notre Dame cathedral.

Paris is the capital of France.
Nearly 3 million people live in Paris
and another 6 million in the many smaller
towns that surround it.

Paris is a city of wide roads, beautiful buildings,
art galleries, museums and parks.

At work

French people work in many different places.
They work in coal and iron ore mines.
They work at gas and oil refineries, and
in factories which build aircraft and cars,
and make electrical goods.

The huge passenger aeroplane called an 'Airbus'
is made in France. This factory is in Toulouse.

This perfume factory makes scented soap which is sold all around the world.

Some people design and make clothes - French fashion is very famous. Designers such as Dior and Chanel have given their names to scent, soaps and make-up, as well as clothes.

Farming

There are many small farms in France.
The farmers grow wheat, barley and oats,
and fruit and vegetables.
They also keep cattle, sheep and poultry.

France is famous for its vineyards
where grapes are grown.
The grapes are used to make wine.

Wine is stored in great wooden barrels before it is put into bottles to be sold.

The milk from the cows – and goats – French farmers keep is often used to make cheese.

Children

These French children are learning how to use computers.

French children live a life
very like yours.
They go to school,
watch television, and
go on trips with their parents.

A visit to EuroDisney
just outside Paris
is a popular trip
for French families.

French food

French cooks are among the best in the world. They often cook with garlic and olive oil. Long sticks of French bread are eaten with most meals.

French people like to eat at restaurants. They sit outside on sunny days.

This man is baking a special French cake called Gateau à la Broche.

Croissants are eaten for breakfast.

Out and about

French people enjoy sport -
cycling, football, riding, rugby
and tennis are all popular.

Boules (a kind of bowls) is played in
town squares all around France.

Children learn to ski when they are very young.
They are often taught in small groups like this one.

French families go skiing in the winter,
usually in the Alps where there is
plenty of snow.

Festivals

Almost every region of France
has its own special festival.

At Le Mans in the Loire valley,
there are festivals to celebrate the motor car.

The most famous car festival at Le Mans has a
24-hour race which goes on all day and all night.

Amazing fruit sculptures are made during Menton's orange and lemon festival.

In Menton on the Mediterranean coast, they have an orange and lemon festival to celebrate the harvest.

Visiting France

Many tourists come on holiday to France.
They come to enjoy its sandy beaches,
and visit its tiny villages and fine towns.
They come to see the exhibitions
in its museums and art galleries.

A glass pyramid stands outside the Louvre in Paris,
once a great palace and now a famous art gallery.

This is *Le Moulin de la Galette* by Auguste Renior (1841–1919), a famous French artist.

Index

About this book

The last decade of the 20th century has been marked by an explosion in communications technology. The effect of this revolution upon the young child should not be underestimated. The television set brings a cascade of ever-changing images from around the world into the home, but the information presented is only on the screen for a few moments before the programme moves on to consider some other issue.

Instant pictures, instant information do not easily satisfy young children's emotional and intellectual needs. Young children take time to assimilate knowledge, to relate what they already know to ideas and information which are new.

The books in this series seek to provide snapshots of everyday life in countries in different parts of the world. The images have been selected to encourage the young reader to look, to question, to talk. Unlike the TV picture, each page can be studied for as long as is necessary and subsequently returned to as a point of reference. For example, a French child's daily life might be compared with their own; a discussion might develop about the ways in which food is prepared and eaten in a country whose culture and customs are different from their own.

The comparison of similarity and difference is the recurring theme in each of the titles in this series. People in different lands are superficially different. Where they live (the climate and terrain) obviously shapes the sort of houses that are built, but people across the world need shelter; coins may look different, but in each country people use money.

At a time when the world seems to be shrinking, it is important for children to be given the opportunity to focus upon those things which are common to all the peoples of the world. By exploring the themes touched upon in the book, children will begin to appreciate that there are strands in the everyday life of human beings which are universal.